FAMOUS LAST WORDS

CATHERINE PIERCE

saturnalia books

Saturnalia Books
13 E. Highland Ave., 2 Floor
Philadelphia, PA 19118
info@saturnaliabooks.com

ISBN: 978-0-9754990-7-8
Library of Congress Control Number: 2007936611

Book Design by Saturnalia Books
Printing by Westcan Printing Group, Canada

Cover Art: Cattle Skull on Fence
© Tim O'Hara / Corbis

Author Photograph: Michael Kardos

Distributed by:
University Press of New England
1 Court Street
Lebanon, NH 03766
800-421-1561

Grateful acknowledgment is made to the publications where these poems first appeared, sometimes in different form: *American Literary Review*: "Advice on Travel"; *Arts and Letters*: "We Are in Love"; *Barrow Street*: "Memphis"; *Bellingham Review*: "Conscience" and "Endearments"; *Blackbird*: "Domesticity" and "This Is Not an Elegy"; *Gulf Coast*: "¿Quien es?"; *Mid-American Review*: "Love Poem to a Blank Space," "Love Poem to Longing," "Love Poem to Sinister Moments," and "Love Poem to the Word *Lonesome*"; *Mississippi Review*: "The man in the photograph"; *Slate*: "Well, gentlemen, you are about to see a baked Appel"; *Smartish Pace*: "This is funny"; *Third Coast*: "Epithalamium"; and *Willow Springs*: "Evolution."

Some of these poems also appear in the chapbook *Animals of Habit* (Kent State University Press, 2004).

"Love Poem to the Word *Lonesome*" and "Love Poem to Sinister Moments" appear in *FlatCity Anthology*, ed. Adam Cole, Kelly McGuinness, and Betsy Wheeler (FlatCity Press, 2005).

"Epithalamium" appears in *Best New Poets 2007*, ed. Natasha Trethewey (Samovar Press, 2007).

My sincere gratitude to the writers, readers, and wonderful friends who in some way helped shape this book, in particular Brian Barker, Nicky Beer, Eddie Christie, Chris Coake, Lauren Kenney, Crystal Lake, Stephanie Lauer, Kelly Magee, Nathan Oates, Michael Piafsky, and Amy Wilkinson. Thanks as well to my teachers at the University of Missouri, the Ohio State University, and Susquehanna University, especially Scott Cairns, Kathy Fagan, Gary Fincke, Michelle Herman, Andrew Hudgins, Lynne McMahon, and Sherod Santos, for their wisdom, support, and friendship. Special thanks to Maggie Smith for her generosity and her unerring eye. Thank you to John Yau, as well as to Henry Israeli at Saturnalia Books. I am deeply grateful to my mother Debbie Albence, my father Carl Pierce, and my sister Sarah Pierce for their love and encouragement. Finally, thank you to Mike Kardos—for every moment.

CONTENTS

I.

Love Poem to Sinister Moments   1
Love Poem to the Word *Lonesome*   3
Love Poem to a Blank Space   4
Love Poem to America   5
Love Poem to the Phrase *Let's get coffee*   6
Love Poem to Doo-Wop   7
Love Poem to Longing   8
Love Poem to Fear   9

II.

Project Yourself Here   13
Domesticity   14
Cross-Country Song   15
While You Sleep, I Watch Myself Die   16
Advice on Travel   17
This Is Not an Elegy   19
Fat Tuesday   21
Retrospect   22
Invention   24
Apostrophe to the First Gray Hair   25
Adolescence   26
We Are in Love   27
Memphis   28
Epithalamium   29
Endearments   30
Why You Love the Annoyances in Your Dreams   31
The man in the photograph   33

In Which I Imagine Myself Into a Western   35
In Which I Imagine Myself Into a Slasher Flick   36
In Which I Imagine Myself Into a Film Noir   37
In Which I Imagine Myself Into a David Lynch Movie   38
The Poem I Cannot Write For You   39
The Heaven I Hope For   40
Graceland   41
Nor Hell a Fury   43
Evolution   44
Postcards Nos. 1-6   45
Conscience   47
Perseids   49
Instinct   50
Ubi Sunt   51

III.
"¿Quien es?"   57
"Well, gentlemen, you are about to see a baked Appel."   58
"Pardonnez-moi, monsieur."   60
"This is funny."   61
"Goodbye, my friends! I go to glory."   62
"Stopped."   64
"Don't let it end like this. Tell them I said something."   65

for Mike

I.

Love Poem to Sinister Moments

You are the dead swan
floating in the Susquehanna.

The red moon before a storm.
You are the series of scars

on a daughter's arm. The tidy
pool of blood on the 7-Eleven counter

and the small white-haired woman
who wipes it away.

You are, when I'm driving,
the sweet smell that may

or may not be poison
gas spilling over the city.

You are cartoons interrupted
by war, the odd-tasting

drink at last call. You are
the gunshots I mistake

for celebration. Lancaster
cornfields, and behind them,

Three Mile Island, smoking
against purple horizon.

Your confidence astounds me.
You arrive uninvited,

grind glass into the pâté, spit
in the gin, and are gone. I want

your perfect broken backbone
for my own. Your long, thin fingers

that always know exactly
which string to pull,

which card will send
the house tumbling down.

LOVE POEM TO THE WORD *LONESOME*

Lonesome, I am pining for you.
You in all your desert-yellow
dryness, your tumbleweed mouth
always open, thirsty. I long

for your cracked hands on me.
Your voice a crying saw. You, so tall
and thin, waiting on the porch
in rags, and me around the corner,

slow-walking. Your coffee, weak.
Your riverbed. Lonesome,
I want your dance-hall girls,
your windburn, your low lights.

I want your single hawk
wheeling overhead, breaking
the sky into pieces.

LOVE POEM TO A BLANK SPACE

You are pure as soil,
simple as bone. The taste

of you transparent. I love
your dumb grace,

your unfelt presence.
The sighs you never

utter. How you know
just when to keep quiet,

when to pretend you don't
notice I'm there. I love

your touch, so light
it hardly happens. How,

when you lean in
to kiss me, it's like kissing

breath, but better:
I know you'll never

go. How when you
open your mouth,

there's nothing at all
inside.

LOVE POEM TO AMERICA

America, teach me how to strut. Teach me
how to whistle with two fingers
in my mouth, how to pop off a bottle cap
with my teeth. You're the one I want

to hate, with all your swagger and bravado,
and of course you take me home
every time. Who could resist? You're the biggest,
blondest movie star of all, the Mr. Universe

of the millennium, your hands and feet
and everything so strong and mindless,
so rugged, *yes*. You're buffalo blood and all things
forbidden, the prizefighter who killed

the favorite fair and square. In bed,
you fell me like a redwood. I'm lost
in your factory body—such perfect and grinding
machinery. Oh, America, you're gritty

and glowing and I love the asphalt taste of you,
your acid smell and your hunger and I love
how, afterward, you roll over and snore
like a locomotive before I even catch my breath.

LOVE POEM TO THE PHRASE *LET'S GET COFFEE*

It's your trickery I love,
your sleek underhandedness,
winking at the start
of so many affairs. I adore
your elegant manners,
one hand on the car door,
the other on the ass.
You don't mess around.
You know the difference
between short and tall,
skim and 2 percent.
You call the shots
in unmistakable code:
chair scraping out,
magazine falling shut,
extra cream, no caffeine,
for the lady. Your designs.
Your calculations. Your one
black eye, winking
through steam at the hand
on the hand on the mug.

LOVE POEM TO DOO-WOP

I can spot you in any crowd—
your suit the bluest, your jaw square

as your shoulders. You glide
oh-so-slowly toward me

in your two-toned loafers, your tie
precise and sincere. I love

how you spin me like a penny
and how, in your hands, I am

small-waisted, torpedo-breasted,
my hair coiffed and sprayed.

You make my pulse shimmy
in the most inappropriate ways.

I love you for how, when I
lean in close and whisper *You make*

my blood lift its skirt above its knees,
you flush the color of light

through streamers and twirl me
to the punch bowl to cool down.

LOVE POEM TO LONGING

Since you've gone,
I've been fine. It's torture.
With you, I was center
ring, always about to fall
from the wire, to drown
in the chained box. I was
the star, with electric
hair, bones of glass. My fragility
kept me suspended.

But now, without you,
what am I? An acrobat
with wings, a diver
with gills, a torch juggler
with fireproof hands?
The tightrope has turned
to sidewalk. I'm not
one to beg, but I need you
back. Your absence will
undo me. You've left me
wanting nothing.

LOVE POEM TO FEAR

Around you, my body is a wire
pulled taut, my jaw a bear-trap
waiting. You have such wicked timing—

arriving just before I drop
into sleep, or worse, when
the one I'm trying to love

is close enough to see me
waver. Then it's questions
and concern, and I feel only

your fingers on my lips, your teeth
against my neck, your smooth-
as-cyanide voice spinning

all your false promises.
Sometimes you vanish
for days. Then, I sleep

till morning, wake against
a shadowless body to clear sky,
green grass, perfect eggs

for breakfast. Those days
I almost forget you. But you're
no gentleman—no warning

and you're back, all bombast
and mystery. Everything
yours for the taking.

II.

PROJECT YOURSELF HERE

A girl stands by a river in central Pennsylvania. Her clothes are vaguely romantic—ragged sneakers caked in mud, a t-shirt worn thin by washings. Is she considering falling in? Does she want someone to think she is considering it? She stands motionless, her shadow pooled about her ankles. It's 8 p.m. in the summer. Red streaks, gold streaks, trees across the water the color of a burning house. And the river itself: wide enough for only a strong swimmer. A current that may or may not relinquish. The girl has no Virginia Woolf fantasies. She is 20 and not foolish, but hasn't yet read Woolf, hasn't yet been horrified and impressed by the stone-in-the-pocket routine. She has a song in her head. You don't know it—it's a local band—but it's about the color yellow and a girl in a field. She wishes she were the girl in a field. But she is the girl by a river. She doesn't think that the girl in a field wishes she were the girl in a Dodge Dart heading west. That the girl in the Dart wishes she were the boy serving drinks in Aspen. That the boy serving drinks wishes he were the man front-porch sitting, rocking away on a street he's never seen, where neighbors love him and bicycle bells ring. She still wants to be a muse. She still wants someone to sneak up and take her picture on black and white film. It would make her glad to know that someone is watching now, even through memory, even through the blue gel of nostalgia. There's more to tell about the girl, but it's better not to know. If you did, you wouldn't want to be her. You wouldn't be remembering how once you were.

DOMESTICITY

Some days I could burn
bookshelves, carve weapons
from the wreckage, drive
fearlessly past dogs and bandits.
I could rocket through towns
of dust. I could destroy
the sheriff's good name.

Then night slips around me
and the bedroom is lit
with a strand of small lights.
My body admits to calm.
I am the same size,
but still. Outside an owl
calls evenly across the quiet,
and I ride that note,
grateful, into sleep.

But this is a warning.
Someday I could drive
the car into the ocean. I could
smash the phone, tear pages
from the dictionary. I could
make threats all my life.
Don't think I won't.

CROSS-COUNTRY SONG

Oh Memphis. Oh Maybell. Oh Hartsburg, MO,
with your one-room winery and your bleak pumpkin
festival. So many knick-knacks. I never wanted
to buy them. Only to be among them. Eight Acre
Lake and pine stillness. There, alien constellations
stud the sky. In Gallup, stunted buttes
and long-dead film stars. In Texas, billboard
swagger, droning heat. Drive on. Old highways
through grain chutes and green. The unfound
ghost town. The one-show Okemah marquee.
In Moab a desert sea of red rock. On Mount Royal
air thin as cobwebs, and silvery at dusk.
Oh country, you are an animal to yourself.
Let me roll in the dust alongside you.

WHILE YOU SLEEP, I WATCH MYSELF DIE

It happens all sorts of ways:
spinal meningitis, a lump I've ignored
for too long, a lung collapsing

sudden as gunshot. My vanishing plays
like a reel-to-reel movie—I never
stop going away. In the library-

quiet of the bedroom, I hear the rush
of sudden stillness, the scrape
of the lowering-down. And so many

details to consider: the embalming,
the makeup, the oak or maple
casket. I want none of it. But

when is it closer than now, our bodies
glistening, the old book smell of sex
still on us? I'm not nearer

to the earth, or ethereal, or holy.
I'm jagged. The next step
could splinter bones and bring me

to my knees. In the corner, the lamp
leans like a crutch. I leave you
dropping through sleep and move

to the window. The moon
shimmers, a placebo. As it falls,
I close my mouth around it.

ADVICE ON TRAVEL

This is what you need: a swift kick
to the head, a hand on your knee
and a suitcase full of wit

and half-formed tales of woe. Get on
the plane that might drop from the sky
like a white anvil. Sit next to the man

with the sinister mole, the ladylike
hands, the perfect blue suit. He might
stalk you from Heathrow to Reykjavik.

He might force you down an icy alley,
leave you minutes later gasping for blood
and sense. Or he could drive you to Piccadilly

where you will see a sleepy version
of *Macbeth* and where the two of you
will, after years of marriage, return.

Leap into the Baltic Sea. It will freeze
your fingers and when ice forms
on the ends of your hair, you will breathe

with clarity. You will not drown, though
you may catch your death days later. But also,
you may not. Give lire to the gypsies who

will steal your wallet, your locket,
your passport. Wear your hair
braided; if they cut it off, the cut

will be even. Hide coins for one call
and one drink in your shoe.
Do not come home until you feel

that if this last plane were to fall, you
could leap from it, buoyed to the ground
by your own great size, the flames below

only another city.

This Is Not an Elegy

At sixteen, I was illegal and brilliant,
my fingernails chewed to half-moons.
I took off my clothes in a late March
field. I had secret car wrecks,
secret hysteria. I sipped anger
and called it cream. In backseats
I learned the alchemy of guilt, lust,
and distance. I was unformed and total.
I swore like a sailor. But slowly the cops
stopped coming around. The heat lifted
its palms. The radio lost some teeth.

Now I see the landscape behind me
as through a Claude glass—
tinted deeper, framed just so, bits
of gilt edging the best parts.
I see my unlined face, a thousand
film stars behind the eyes. I was
every murderess, every whip-
thin alcoholic, every heroine
with the silver tongue. Always young
Paul Newman's best girl. Always
a lightning sky behind each kiss.

Some days I watch myself
in the third person, speak to her
in the second. I say: I will
meet you in sleep. I will know you
by your stillness and your shaking.

By your second-hand gown.
By your bruises left by mouths
since forgotten. This is not
an elegy because I cannot bear
for it to be. It is only a tree branch
against the window. It is only a cherry
tomato slowly reddening in the garden.
I will put it in my mouth. It will
be sweet, and you will swallow.

FAT TUESDAY

Down on Canal amid masks and dark
the cat-girl's heart opens into the street.

No one notices; people revolve through
the liquor mart like soldiers. In an alley,

one man kneels before another. They love
each other. One has given the other

rare purple beads. A girl joins them
and they welcome her like a daughter.

Women have had their breasts painted
like delicate moths. In the dark they look

clothed. In the dark they look hungry.
At the other end of the Quarter, a woman

dressed in red sings in a black-red bar.
She collects change in a jar and performs

Elvis tunes in Portuguese. She is a house
favorite. A man sits beneath the table.

He imagines he is home, in the snow,
somewhere he has always hated. He has

no lover, but will find one. He will slouch
with purpose toward Canal. The cat-girl

will watch him with glassed eyes. She is housed
now in sleep. The city has given her up.

RETROSPECT

Remember Moab, Utah. The red
rock light and the reservoir where you

plunged into cold and burst out
shivering, schools of silver desert fish

around you. Be careful
with your memory. It was not

deliverance. At the time,
you felt no relief. Just small, tight

breaths of happiness, or what
you thought happiness might be.

Remember the two hours it took
to pitch the borrowed tent, how

afterward two rods lay unused
in the sand. In retrospect,

this is funny. But then you felt
only a slight stir of the fear

you'd been riding for months.
Remember the watery beer,

$3.80 for a six-pack at the gas station
in town. The joint packed in the toe

of your sneaker, and how
you watched an airplane spin

in tight circles and wondered what,
exactly, you were smoking.

And here your memory and
the night have no quarrel:

You lay back on the cold rock,
watching the living sky, your hands

moving over your own body, slow
as water. You wanted to drift up

into the cask of stars. But
in the lake you'd felt small

nips of near joy. So
you pressed your hands

hard to your body and waited.
If you had to hold yourself down

to stay here, then you would.

INVENTION

The Wild says the sign. Humming red
against black-blue sky. The next word
burnt out, bulbs black
against the bar door. The girl
who dreams the sign wants
not to know the next word.

In *The Wild* are songs and rough manners
to live by. There she could press
herself against a man and swirl down
his throat like whiskey. She could
sway with him over the state line
to Arkansas. She could—

(and she knows how invention works.
She knows there's no place for salvation.
That whiskey is a movie man's drink.
That rough manners mean bellows,
not eloquence. She knows she knows—)

But she shakes her head (with tangles
like curls that must break
anyone's heart). Nothing in her ear
but the record's warm scratching,
the man's low voice. *The Wild*

says the sign. If she listens hard
she can enter it. She can
dissolve into the humming words
that still might be her.

APOSTROPHE TO THE FIRST GRAY HAIR

O small silver rope by whose noose
I will, if lucky, hang—

You are the highway's white stripe
dividing *toward* from *away*.

The hairline fracture
on a slowly swaying bridge.

Light plummeting earthward
years after the star has turned dark.

ADOLESCENCE

The girls are the words
from the stories: *willowy, lissome, lithe.*
Their hair *black as ebony wood*, or
fine as spun gold. They have gifts.
Voices like water. They move like light

through leaves. But in the world
you imagine, you have your own story.
Your name is *Vivienne* (or *Eva*,
Lavinia; there must be Vs
and hints of red). You dream yourself

into every fairytale, the grisly
versions where the prince's eyes
run blood and the girl disappears
into the wolf's dark throat.
You understand the good

must be punished, and this is why
you would be neither
the red-capped girl nor the princess
in the briar-wrapped tower,
but the queen whose word

is *wicked*, who conjures smoke
and poison. You would know the forest
in the dark. You were meant
to wear beasts' pelts. To lure
the golden girl to your spinning wheel.

You have no sister like a rose,
no brother to lead you out.
What you have: a castle
to yourself. A lying mirror.
A bear's heart, salted, on a plate.

WE ARE IN LOVE

after Diane Arbus

He's tall enough, hair a sharp bay wave.
If I were sixteen, we'd be married. But for now
we walk down Hudson Street, not even cold,
me in my Ann-Margret coat and his mouth
sweet as Eddie Fisher's, but tough. We know
we will be famous. We carve our initials
in cement and no one catches us. In Woolworth's
we stuff our pockets with cigarettes and cherry candy.
No one sees; we're quick, and look like we belong
anywhere we go. See his neat tie, his eyes
that catch whatever approaches. We've got plans.
Big money, big times. We'll knock this world out.
Already our hands are like bricks.

MEMPHIS

You've held all you could hold: rhythms
that shook the ground, shook men's hips,

shook screams loose from pale-lipped girls.
Flood waters rising. Gunshots that spun

a country off its axis, and then just
silence like centuries falling away. Now

you're airbrushed ties and five-dollar
Cokes, neon flashing the names

of your buried sons. You're scaffolding,
mere frame of yourself. You hide

behind cheap harmonicas and cheaper
daiquiris, and I love you for this,

and for how each street leads halfway
into the past and dead ends in an alley

where a skinny girl sings "Milk Cow Blues"
gravely, with too much grace. You're tired.

If I could, I would sway you to dreaming,
movement slow and easy as a railroad car.

But each night you blaze with the ghosts
of all you've lost. They rise from storefronts

and bars, from the Peabody and the trees
behind Graceland. They light the sky

like a radio dial. They need you still.

EPITHALAMIUM

First, know the type of car the other drove
as a high school senior, late eighties. Were there
bucket seats? Red interior? You must love
that car. You must wish, at least briefly, that you
had ridden in it. Next, you must understand
the psychology of the belt buckle and the black boots.
They were chosen for a reason. Know that reason
and never speak of it. Purchase for each other
not only books and dinners, but plastic
serving trays, origami kits, a postcard from Tupelo
to be hand-delivered, unmarked. Be kind to old
photographs, but not overly kind. Know the name
of a town in Mexico where you can someday,
money willing, spend a week. Consider starting
a four-piece cover band. Consider growing
basil and/or marijuana. Know that at no point
do you have to own a) tapered jeans, b) a good blender,
c) spare light bulbs. These are your decisions to make.
Remember small parts of many days: the Amish
restaurant outside the city. The purchase of the red vase.
The bird whose cries woke you your first morning
in one bed. How you rose together then.

ENDEARMENTS

You are my gloaming. My lucky
number. You are my fortune
cookie. I name you ostrich, beanbag,
lump. I name you matchbox. Never
go, my homing pigeon. Stay
and keep me warm, my wooly
glove, my teapot. It's difficult
these days to say anything
new. All the more reason to love
you, my air conditioner, my Model-
T. You keep everything humming.
You're my little French phrase, my
*Je crois que j'ai un abcès**, my sweet, sweet
nasal vowel. You're my desk lamp.
Never forget me, my elephant. Never
run off, my Flo Jo, my Maserati. Oh,
dear almanac, dear Catholic church,
dear hatbox-in-the-sky, just promise
you'll call me *Forever*.

* I think I have an abscess

Why You Love the Annoyances in Your Dreams

You can't get your basketball shoes laced.
When you do, the game is nearly over
and you've just realized you're late

for a Spanish final. When you reach
the classroom, you remember you dropped
Spanish three months ago. You rush back

to the game, which has just wrapped up. Then
you're at a conference, but the conference
is in Schenectady and it's March. Also,

the hotel bathroom is covered in cat fur.
Gross, you say. You can't find
the number for your friend's room

and when you do he is that kid
from sixth grade who stole your copy
of *The Hobbit* and called you troll boy.

He wears a business suit and is marginally
successful. He busts you about old times
and on your way out you stub your toe.

In dreams, these annoyances are epic.
Your stomach twists; your teeth grind. And
you love them for this. Even in sleep, you know

that once you drop like a rock into waking,
everything will shift. In your daytime world,
when your car stalls on I-70, or you miss

the big deadline, or the cat runs out of food
during the county's biggest snowstorm
since '94, even as you pound your steering wheel,

even then, you'll know all too well
that these are your life's small highlights.
You're just biding time until the tragedies.

Soon, your wife will take the day off,
make the bed with perfect hospital
corners, and vanish for Cabo.

You'll feel a lump in some never-before-
considered spot. Your mother will fall
and shatter her hip and your sister

will call you, frantic and frightened, but
you'll be across the country
at a conference in Schenectady, New York,

with no one to shake you awake and say,
what a bummer of a night for you, but
it's morning now, wake up, it's morning.

The Man in the Photograph

is the man in every photograph,
not foregrounded, but highlighted,
the only one in the packed, smoky room
looking straight at the camera. He is the one
your gaze veers to always, distracted
from the laughing couple veiled under rice,
the Texas air show, your grandparents waving
from their cruise ship's deck.

He is the same man in the crowd
scene in every movie, head tilted back,
smoking on the street corner. He catches
your eye while young Robert Redford—
too moral and ruddy and smug—
holds forth. When the light turns
and he crosses out of frame, you miss him.

He is the man who sits alone
in every good dark bar in every country
not your own. You hope his eyes are on you
as you order your vodka straight, no ice.
You hope he's watching as the music
makes you sad. You walk past his table
on your way to the bar and he's gone.

If he were a Cuban rebel, profiled
against the knotted underbrush, a broker
in the back corner of the NYSE,
a weary Czechoslovakian cellist

in his city's only dancehall, it wouldn't matter;
you would know him. You would lean
toward him through the close, dim air.
By the time you got near enough
to say his name, the film would be over,
the album snapped shut, the bar lights
up and blinding.

In Which I Imagine Myself Into a Western

Come. Take my hand,
rough from fields. Yonder
the sun sets, molten, unhinged.
I'll drink whiskey with you.
I'll sing you a murder ballad.
With me you put down
the gun, undo my petticoat.
The moon a noose behind us.

In Which I Imagine Myself Into a Slasher Flick

The Jennies get it first.
The Trishes. The Ambers.
Never my silhouette through
shower steam. Never my red
mouth in close-up. I've got
straight As and no boyfriend.
I've got Friday nights
and sleeping neighbor children.
But worry. Because I've got
an unadorned name. Sharp
vision by moonlight.
My father's rusted hatchet
and a jetliner scream.

In Which I Imagine Myself Into a Film Noir

What I love is to be behind things—
opaque glass doors. Smoke
rings drifting like fog. Dark glasses
large as eclipses. Schemes.
Leave your hat on. It casts
a distinctive shadow.
All the way down
the oil-slicked alley
I can watch you
watch me.

In Which I Imagine Myself Into a David Lynch Movie

I am the girl in your dreams.
I wear a cocktail dress and dirt
in my teeth. For you, my exquisite
doom. For you, this aching
music, this blue-smoked diner,
this careful lipstick blood.
Make me famous. But don't
wake up. At dawn,
mechanical birds sing hollow
through your night-wrecked
and blissful town.

THE POEM I CANNOT WRITE FOR YOU

is meteors above an August cornfield.
Or L.A. in a rented car. It's what

we loved without admitting it, and all
you've since forgotten. Sly, this poem, and tricky—

it kneels beside you while you sleep, spins details
into dreams you can't quite shake. The poem

remembers what you've overlooked: coyotes
on a matchbook, sugared pears, the rattle

your car made for a week last fall. It hands
each moment, small and silver-wrapped, to you.

The poem knows your days are pocked with loss,
riddled with missing nights and vacancies.

It knows that you don't notice, that your rooms
and hands stay full. But this is not enough,

and so the poem gives back what you've misplaced:
your keys, your favorite hat, the red umbrella.

December, and our breath a cloud of sparks.

The Heaven I Hope For

is a sky-wide room with four corners:
the garden, Ted's Bar, Tahoe, bed.

I'll swim from the dark red light
of Ted's right into alpine air. Mud

in my hair from planting. Pear tomatoes
yellow against the lake's glass-blue glare.

I'll hike through black-eyed aspen
drunk on dark rum, jukebox humming

from the sky. All night I'll pot basil
and thyme beneath mountain stars,

water far below, and caps of snow
on the highest highball. And after

the pines and smoky inclines,
after noon bar darkness

and the cool radish moon: a bed,
enormous and smooth as a gin

lake. I'll dream myself drowned
in dirt. Then I'll rise like wild mint.

GRACELAND

is full of high school kids,
angled and angry, who've come
to see the golden jumpsuit.

They want pictures
with the fur-lined bed, the den
of seaweed shag. They want Love

Me Tender snow globes and pens,
the perfect shimmering necktie,
postcards with his bloated eyes

to send to friends back east.
Their parents never explained.
The kids don't know

that their fathers wept when
he was found, their mothers
fought screams. They never

saw him, all ass and knees
and mouth, break TVs to pieces
while the girls cried and cried.

They know only the radio song
in their mothers' Volvos,
the Technicolor movies

their fathers watch late at night.
They know only his black
pompadour, the snarl they've mirrored

in charades. The kids tour
the house, see the gold
records, the acrylic paintings

done by fans. They watch
grandmothers drag toddlers
through room after room

of display cases and spotlights.
The kids begin to wonder
why they came. It's tough

to laugh, though they do.
When they reach the graves,
the sky sweats. They compose

their faces carefully. No one
can tell what they're thinking.
They feel a strange weight,

their legs suddenly concrete.
Their stomachs sink. *Fuck
that*, they say. They know

someday they'll be left.
Their former selves
luminous and gone.

NOR HELL A FURY

I am the step that creaks.
The window that slams shut.
I am the one rough spot
on the smooth broom handle;
I'll lodge in your palm,
a stranger. I am the wrong perfume
in your hair. I am the rusty can.
The fishhook at the bottom
of the lake, and your foot
drifting down like a leaf.
Do you know how many
have ended this way—
crippled, one hand useless?
You think I'm nothing more
than mites in the cat's ear,
static crackling the phone. But
I'm the gasoline in the garage
and the cigarette you tossed. Darling,
when your wife wakes
as you creep into bed, I'm
the hush she doesn't recognize
announcing you like fanfare.

EVOLUTION

You wake to coffee and your lover says, *It's just over.*
Yet everything smells the same. He goes, and you lust over

all hot things: the bacon in the pan, the shower steam.
The dishes pile in the sink. The cat fattens and the dust over

light bulbs builds. You drift about, ignore the phone.
You don't drive much. The hubcaps begin to rust over.

You should shower, buy groceries, but still, there's some appeal to this:
the tangled hair, the quivering. You inspire intrigue, not disgust. Over-

night, it seems, the garden bursts into saffron and ruby.
You decide you're evolving, and it's hard, but you must. Over

time, you will become feral and bright as the weeds. You glow
and preen. Once, your lover drops by. He is thin, but you've fussed over

him enough, and besides, he asks the wrong questions. You smile
and nod. You are polite but reticent. He seems nonplussed over

the smallest things: the garden, your hair like larkspur. That night,
winter drops its hammer. You watch dry wood combust. Over

the crack of the door, the wind is a siren. Soon it snows. Icicles
pierce the light. Whiteness. The windows crust over.

Postcards Nos. 1-6

4.17

I'm supposed to say *wish you were here*. Or *the water's swell*. Or what have you. But what with the pine and the oily lake, this is better. What with the teakettle whistling. What with the sound the door makes when it opens to no one.

Don't forget to sleep.

xo,
X

6.24

Did I tell you about the last time my parents were in the same room? I was there. Or at least I've imagined it. They stared at each other. Four dead fish eyes and me the color of wallpaper. I waited for one of them to vaporize the other. But no one had the energy. Your tomatoes must be in the ground by now. They must be fruiting. Did you plant the ugly ones again? Are they tart like last year?

X

7.4

It's a picnic day. Will you color your hair blue? Did you ever, when you were a kid? Was there a cookout, and did you eat too many hotdogs and curl into your mother's lap, and did she tell you it would be okay? And was it?

Forgive me. I sound frantic. I'm not. Does that worry you?

xxxxx,
X

7.5
It worries me.

8.19
If I come back, let's go to the Cadillac Ranch. It's in Amarillo. I saw it once—Cadillacs nosing out of the ground like dolphins. There are seven, I think, or nine. Everyone scrawls love and proclamations on them. If we go, I want you to paint my name there. I've painted yours here.

All my frustration,
X

10.1
Or to Alaska. We could see caribou and wolverines. We could stay awake for days. So much light. Would it drive us crazy, do you think? Is it cold even in the summer? Know that if I could I would apologize. If I could I would slip under the crack of your door and fall into bed with you like someone almost drowned. But I don't have enough words. And can't fit through small spaces. I am running out of room. Come to the bus depot. Bring your helmet. And your arrows. I will be the girl wearing nothing.

Yours, most likely,
X

Conscience

"The owner of a fish hatchery has been charged with killing 4,000 endangered or protected birds and an alligator, police said."
— CNN online

In one year, my workers shot
through egrets, meadowlarks,
black-neck stilts. The birds
helicoptered into the bayou
from the thick Florida sky,
fabulous in death, their wings
shut tight as doors. I cannot tell you
how I hate them. How the air
around them sours. Too many
times, the pitiful flop of silver
in hooked beak, the dumb, trusting
eyes locked into watching. And then
the blood like a movie—it slips
from the split bodies,
splashes like a solid thing.

I've stayed quiet when
the reporters ask questions.
Let them think it was job
security. Let them think
it was selfish. I won't
tell them how, each night,
I heard strange, watery echoes
made by mouths submerged,
a long, high keening
that stiffened my spine.

I won't tell them what I saw
behind my eyes: fish bones
falling from clouds.

Now my husband pays bail,
mystified. But I know
what I've done. For the rest
of my life, I will dream
silver schools, soft beds
of eggs. I will sleep
like a woman underwater.

PERSEIDS

The details we share in memory:
It was mid-August. What we felt was not
yet language. You brought two cans
of MGD and I drove us out of town.
Your plan: primary road to secondary,
then, when the city's orange glow was gone,
a tertiary turn. We rumbled over gravel
between waves of dark corn. A hound howled.
We shared one beer and did not touch.
We lay on the hood of my car and watched
small white balls streak across the sky,
slower than we expected.

A detail you do not know:
That dog sounded to me like the dog
that precedes a gunshot. It seemed
utterly possible that a farmer
would come out of that lit house
on the dark horizon and cock
a rifle. That we'd meet Midwestern
justice unfiltered. And I realized
nothing just then. Death there,
amid the high swaying corn, under slow
rockets of light, with you warm next to me
against the summer chill held
no appeal. Here was no August epiphany.
But we drank our beer. We watched
long enough, while the hound bayed
over the fields and no one came out.
This night was just one night. Everything
slower than we expected.

INSTINCT

I woke to screaming. Outside, a raccoon
was opening a cat. The cat shrieked like a child
as red ropes spooled from its belly.
There was nothing to do; it couldn't
be saved, was already beginning
to shudder. After another minute,
it was still, its entrails steaming
in the crisp air. The raccoon
waddled away, uninterested.

This is a love poem.
It isn't about the cat or the raccoon.
It's about you, still asleep, breathing
evenly and guiltless, and me, awake
and fascinated. What do you see, sleeping?
Empty hallways, maybe, or broken
bottles, or gardens of flesh blooming
around bullets. You could pull
so many triggers behind your eyes. Or maybe
just a woman, tall, with thin wrists. How easily
I could leave you, slip on my coat and shoes
while you dream of what I can't know. So simple

to kill what we don't understand. But instead
we allow it. We sleep next to each other,
roll over at three a.m. and startle
at the weight that balances our bed. We could
spend a lifetime circling, sniffing each other out,
and then turn to meet a dark, clawed creature
we've never seen but know like we know
our bones. Nothing can alter our course. We are animals
of habit. We shut our bodies down together,
wake each morning gutted and hungry.

Ubi Sunt

Once, we were trespassers. All night
we hid in the graveyard, on the trestle,
on the dock that rocked while dark
birds floated past. We were glad then
in our sadness. Chilled, we watched
the sky for constellations we could name.

Once, we were voyagers. Smoky trains
chugged through other countries, green fields
ratcheting by in Rothko blocks. We wove
weeds through our hair. We hummed
Neil Young in metro stations, got locked
on hotel roofs, wrote cryptic postcards home.

Once, we were earthquakes. We wore
boots and lashes and clouds of aerosol.
We imagined the applause was sincere.
We had teacup faces and cyclone minds.
In the backstage quiet we learned how
to talk dirty, how to suffer with abandon,
how to make our wise mothers worry.

Sometimes we were dust motes, mute
with small shock when the cat died
in the house fire, when we first heard
our howls, bottomless, butcher-block red.
Sometimes—when the phone rang
too late, when the liquor ran out, when
our fists became white-knuckled rocks—
we were whirling mirror balls.

Now, we seldom tremble, seldom howl,
our trespasses glaring in their rarity. We are
full-tanked cars on a clean black highway.
But once we were lost in a deep wood.
Once, songs fell into our hands like strands
of diamonds. We were sword-swallowers
then, and we weren't afraid.

III.

"¿QUIEN ES?"

—last words of Billy the Kid

Sawdust. Dark rivers winding
through it and his own hand a raft.
This sudden thirst. And a pounding
coming toward him, an animal
bellowing, and something warm
across his throat, feathery
as pollen. He cannot say who
the boots belong to. He thinks,
what a sudden sleep.

He will wake tomorrow
and tell the story of how
he almost vanished. Breakfast
of griddlecakes, fried eggs, steak. Then
he will get on the piebald and steal
the next girl he sees. She will ring
like a silver bell. He will love her
right to water.

Or it is morning already, light
against his eyelids like a blade.
And the girl has come, rosed
and braided, done up like a painting.
She eddies into the bright place.
He holds his breath to follow
under and down.

"WELL, GENTLEMEN, YOU ARE ABOUT TO SEE A BAKED APPEL."

—last words of gangster George Appel, before being put to
death by electric chair

Each time his girl visited, lips pressed
like stained tulips, cheeks pinched
into heat for the man behind the glass,
she left shaking her head, scuffing
her Sunday shoes against the pavement.

Why did she believe this time
might be different? That this morning
he might remember her breasts beneath
the winter coat, the nub of her earlobe
in his teeth? All he watched for now

was the expression of her mouth.
What about this, he'd say. *What's cooking?*
Or *How about you fry up something good?*
Then he'd grin and say *I'm on fire!*
Electric, even. At first, the girl wept,

chewed her nails—he was hysterical,
surely raped and maddened in that cell.
But each imagined rimshot carried her
further from her wedding,
her sand-white dress, solid hands

around her waist. She tried,
she told her mother. She brought
caramels, pinups, photographs of herself
naked, and he would say *I got a good one
today. What do you call a fruit in a chair?*

What do you get when you cross...
She threatened to stop coming. But
each time he would beg, his face drooping
like a wet stocking. When the day came,
the girl was there, eyes swollen, hands nervous.

She heard the words, then silence broken
only by his choked laugh, the laugh
broken by the current. In bed that night
she would not tell him how the orderlies
wheeled the gurney in. How,

when they strapped him on, no one
made a sound. She would tell him instead
about the guards doubling over, the priest bowing
into his grin. The whole gray room vibrating
with the aftershock of his wit.

"PARDONNEZ-MOI, MONSIEUR."

—last words of Marie Antoinette, upon stepping on
her executioner's foot

Here is the scaffold. Here
the yelping crowd, the pink
women with their hair spilling
from terrible hats, the men
with the missing teeth, goatish
grins. Nine months earlier,
her husband's head dropped
into this same straw basket. Now
she will follow him along
this slow current of taunts,
the jeers that pulse like the blood
she knows will still pump
one, two, three seconds after.
She has been bound; her hair,
now the color of dirty snow,
has been cut with dull scissors.
At the platform, the bayonets
line her periphery, the faces
a blur of pig-flesh, rat-eyes.

It isn't forgiveness she seeks.
It isn't grace. It's simply the feel
of those six syllables she
has carried all her life, lips
pressed together, tongue warm
against the roof of the mouth. And this
last sound, deep in the throat,
like a winged insect buzzing.
She kneels down. Sets it free.

"This is funny."
—last words of Doc Holliday

Not the whiskey, though that, too,
had its moments. Not the end

of the delirium, not the late afternoon
light languishing across the bed

red as cactus flowers. Not the way
he both recognized and didn't

each face around him. And not
this movement toward sleep,

this motion he could not stop
even if he tried, pulling him

like a riptide toward the shuttering.
What he saw was a black-eyed,

whore-fat bird, landing on the sill
with half a worm in its hooked beak.

The bit of worm flopped like a fish
and he thought *That worm half is half*

alive. The whiskey warmed him,
the light bloomed, the faces

went quiet, and he died laughing,
watching the bird swallow

his life, pieced and thrashing.

"Goodbye, my friends! I go to glory."

—last words of Isadora Duncan. As her car drove away from
the party, her long scarf wrapped around a back wheel and
strangled her.

Surely she said something else
before it happened. After shutting
the car door, did she say to the driver

Ivan, the moon is a fish eye tonight,
let's watch it from the seashore, or
Darling, I adore your cufflinks?

Did she complain of a touch
of indigestion—*The deviled eggs*
were beyond the pale, I'm afraid?

Did she cough? Hiccup? We can't
dare believe she may have belched,
or sworn at her pinching sandals—

Oh, these damn bastard shoes! No,
we love her because the last words
that we know confirm what we knew—

that she spoke in rapturous archaisms,
that she had lilted and gauzed
through some century from which no

photographs exist. We love her
because, when she bade a farewell
we can only describe as gay,

she didn't know she was in earnest.
In her plan for the evening, glory
may have been the green-lit wine café

on the other side of town. It might
have been the seaside, where she
and this driver could collapse

on the sand, drape themselves
into the most classic of shapes
at the water's foaming edge.

Or maybe glory was intended to be
a bed in a quiet flat five stories
above the city. Let's imagine the bed

four-postered. Let's surround it
with marble statues, fig trees, grape leaves
dipped in gold. Let's imagine her

reaching it that night, spinning herself
into it as it casts forward in the dark,
a ship across the Aegean toward sleep.

"STOPPED."

—last word of Joseph Henry Green, 19th century physician,
spoken after taking his own pulse

He's seen his share of dying. The indications vary—sometimes
a shudder, sometimes a clenching of knuckle-white hands—

but always, there is confusion. A vision of a long-dead mother
or sister. Once, of a pet dog (*O Cinders, you've come home!* He cringes

even now). Once, of a mistress. He has watched the dying cower
as lantern shadows flutter into bats, as the loved aunt's portrait expands

to God's fearsome visage. So now, seeing no spiders on the duvet,
no childhood sweetheart waltzing in the corner, he is calm.

His brain feels to him like a well-made watch. He recognizes
his thin-faced wife, his son, bald as an egg, the pastor

from St. Someone of Something, there at his worried wife's behest.
He has refused a doctor. *If I can't diagnose myself, I am too far gone*

to save. But he could recite the recipe for split pea soup (*ham bone,
salt pork, six cups water*). He could quote passages from Genesis

(*There were giants in the Earth in those days; and also after that*). His wife
thinks he is lost, but he will prove himself. His breath rattles

like marbles in a cup. He places two fingers against his wrist
and waits for his blood's report. Beyond his son's thick frame,

he watches a small patch of sky open like a pocket.

"DON'T LET IT END LIKE THIS. TELL THEM I SAID SOMETHING."

—last words of Pancho Villa

Make it up. Let it unfold from his parched,
dusted lips. Let him die cinematically.
Let his men gather round him.

> *Nothing ever vanishes.*

Or:

> *Over there—see?—dawn.*

List them:

> *The earth opens her palms to me.*

> *I have loved my country, and I will.*

> *What else can one man do?*

But he bloodied the countryside. Is rumored
to have killed to fulfill a thirst, to have shot the priest
who begged for mercy. Do we serve him thus?

> *Fuck the dogs.*

> *Kill them for me.*

> *Stop the car, you mongrel, stop.*

Still, he led armies to protect his people.
Gave land to fallen men's widows.

Did not drink, and danced till moonset
with the women of the camp.

The clouds part for me.

Emilio, bless you.

Open the door so I can see the mountains.

It is too much responsibility.
In making words, we make a life. We cannot
give you the conclusion you wanted.

All we know:
You died by gunfire.
You saved and broke hundreds.
It was too late for you.

We know you did not say:

Water.

It is very difficult.

It is not like sleep.

Please.

But we cannot help but imagine. Forgive us—
our efforts are not for you. You understand
the need for the right words. How else
can we live forever? How else
can we write ourselves in?